T0203455

For further information, contact

Tumblehome, Inc.
201 Newbury St., #201
Boston, MA 02116
https://tumblehomebooks.org/

ISBN-13 978-1-943431-58-8
ISBN-10 1-943431-58-2
Library of Congress Control Number 2024941536

Monteith, Barnas
Get Ready for A.I. / Barnas Monteith—1st ed

Printed in Taiwan

10 9 8 7 6 5 4 3 2 1

Tumblehome, Inc.

Get
Ready
For

A.I.

a young reader's guide to
artificial intelligence

Barnas Monteith

Contents

Intro

A.I. is artificial intelligence—intelligence in a machine. But what is intelligence? When you think about the word intelligence, what does it really mean to you?

Does it mean that something or someone is really smart, or does it have a different meaning? Let's take an example—if you think about a pet dog that somehow always knows how to retrieve a particular tennis ball, would you say that the dog is smart? How about dolphins and whales that can communicate with each other using sounds underwater? Or how about some chimpanzees and gorillas who not only know how to make and use tools to find food, but can even learn to use sign language? Are they intelligent?

In fact, yes, these are all examples of natural intelligence in the animal world. Of course, we humans possess plenty of intelligence too. We have the ability to learn new skills, think in a logical way, remember things, and adapt to new environments. Humans have been able to become the top species in nearly every environment in the world. Humans, unlike other animals, can adapt to environments far beyond normal human conditions. We have achieved supersonic flight, dived down to the deepest parts of the ocean—and even travelled to the moon and back. And a lot more!

For many of these feats, we have had the help of machines. But most of these machines are not intelligent. Humanity has managed most of the major technological accomplishments of the past century without the use of A.I.. While it may seem that some machines, such as planes, submarines, and spacecraft, are "smart" in one way or another, most of them in the past have relied primarily on "automation." These are features of the machines that perform a task in response to an outside input. Humans set up the machines to do specific things, and humans make all the decisions. The machines are directed by human intelligence.

In more recent times, however, as we ask machines to perform more complex tasks, such as steering a car past obstacles, human engineers often turn to artificial intelligence. A.I. can improve performance and safety, and increasingly it is achieving things we never imagined. It is important to understand the big difference between automation and intelligence. Sometimes this can be tricky, and we will get into this in more detail in later chapters.

However, in this book we talk about the potential of intelligence in computers and machines. Machines that can learn and think, perhaps one day even entirely on their own. Computer scientists, hardware engineers and other people who work in artificial intelligence use natural intelligence, specifically human intelligence, as the example to guide their own work. That is to say, natural intelligence and artificial intelligence are similar in many ways, and computers can do more and more things that humans can do—plus a lot more that we can't. Reports of remarkable A.I. breakthroughs are coming out every day, at a constantly increasing pace.

Imagine a world where all your daily tasks are assisted by a smart robot. Your homework could be assisted by an at-home computer-based tutor, at a pace of learning that feels comfortable for you, with lots of kind words when you answer a question correctly. Your ride to school on the bus would be replaced by a smart, self-driving car that weaves in and out of traffic quickly as it chooses the safest route to school. Your breakfast would automatically be made for you in minutes if you just say, "Hmmm, I think I'd like to have scrambled eggs and waffles with strawberries and maple syrup today." Your personal robotic assistant could help you "virtually" try on different clothes in the morning. And once you decided which clothes to wear, your robot would retrieve them for you, so you don't have to rummage through your drawers to find clean matched socks yourself. Not to mention, your assistant would wash all your dirty clothes and make sure that your room is clean by the time you get home from school. Without you ever having to lift a finger. The things that you, your parents, bus drivers, afterschool tutors, or other people normally do for you could simply be done by smart machines.

Would this be better than your life today? Most definitely! Just maybe, when a computer did these things for you, your parents and tutors would get to have a little break, and you would get to have things the way you want with a lot less work. Everything would be just a little faster and a little easier. You and other people in your life would have more time to do the other things in life you really want to do.

Having it your way is certainly one very appealing aspect of the potential of A.I., but there is so much more to discuss in later chapters. But of course, with every new technology, there may be drawbacks. For instance, what happens to the bus driver or tutor whose job is no longer needed? Will A.I. replace these people in the future? While some people may benefit from these applications of A.I., others may not. These are things to think about when developing new A.I. technologies, or any technology for that matter.

A.I. is not just one thing or one idea. It's not just about programming or computers. It is a highly cross-disciplinary field of study, involving different fields of science, engineering/technology and math. Many of today's top A.I. labs employ more than just scientists and engineers, often including people from a wide variety of different backgrounds. That is because developing great A.I. is not just about knowing lots of programming languages, or having great math skills, or understanding complex computer hardware. A.I. calls upon different areas of human expertise. Some of the many areas of study that have benefitted from the giant leaps in A.I. in recent years include medicine, agriculture, and energy, to name just a few. These are fields that are important to the survival of all humans.

To be sure, A.I. still falls far short of being truly competitive with the human mind. Still, there are more and more indications that machine learning and artificial intelligence are well on their way to a period of accelerated innovation. A few decades ago, many people questioned whether a world with truly intelligent machines was even possible. But, today, in the minds of many scientists and engineers, it is no longer a question of how, but when, machines become smarter than the people who invented them. It's an incredibly exciting time for the field of artificial intelligence.

Are you ready for A.I.?

Why A.I.?

People have always fantasized about a world with smart helpers to assist in daily human tasks. From the earliest days of humanity, people domesticated animals and developed machines to make life easier. Throughout history, people have wondered what life would be like if they had automatic helpers to assist with everyday tasks.

One early example of this is a story from hundreds of years ago, thought to be one of the earliest conceptions of a robot-like being with its own form of intelligence. It is the story of the Golem, well known in Jewish culture. This mythical creature appears in numerous legends, but there is one in particular, originally told hundreds of years ago in Prague, Czech Republic, that feels familiar today. According to one version of this tale, at that time, the city was in much need of water. So a wise rabbi created a humanoid figure, named the "Golem," out of clay. It came to life (through supernatural magic, of course, not robotic mechanisms and software), and its maker instructed it to fetch water from the Vltava River and carry it into the city. The Golem was instructed how to retrieve a bucket of water and empty it at a certain location, and to repeat this task over and over again. The idea to create a robot-like creature to help perform this much-needed task was certainly a good one. However, the Golem was never "programmed" about when to stop, and before long, the city was flooded with water. While smart enough to help humans perform a mundane task, it unfortunately was not intelligent enough to know when to stop retrieving water.

A Prague reproduction of the Golem

A similar story, which you may have seen, appeared hundreds of years later in a 1940 Disney film called *Fantasia* (based on a German poem by Goethe). In the film, Mickey Mouse is working as an apprentice to a Sorcerer. The Sorcerer gives Mickey the nearly identical job of retrieving water in a bucket from one part of the castle and dumping it into a well in another part of the castle. After Mickey gets tired of this dull and repetitive task, he performs a magic spell on a nearby broom and trains it to perform this job in his place. Sadly, the outcome is similar to the Golem story. The castle becomes completely flooded, and Mickey is in big trouble.

Both these stories seem written to teach a moral lesson—not to take shortcuts in life, and to do your own work. But the reality is, if the Golem or Mickey's broomstick had been designed to be a little smarter and had retrieved exactly the right amount of water, everything would have worked out just perfectly. Of course, that wouldn't leave the reader with much of a moral. But the story could still be great for starting a discussion of the ideas behind developing practical artificial intelligence-based applications.

There are valuable computer science lessons in these stories too. In software programming, the primary problem in both the Golem and Fantasia examples is something we would call an "infinite loop," which is a coding mistake that causes portions of programs to run again and again, endlessly. Without a way to break this loop, in both cases, we ended up with a massive flood. While most infinite loops don't cause giant floods, they can certainly cause computers to freeze, or at least make it hard to stop a particular program. One way to stop a loop is to set some pre-defined parameters. For example, you could ask the Golem or the broomstick retrieve a fixed number of buckets full of water, for instance a number like ten. If we were to represent this as a program written in Python (which is one of the most favored/popular languages for A.I. programs these days), we might represent it like this:

Ideal Golem/Broomstick Python Program

```
1. Bucket_of_water = 0
2. while Bucket_of_water < 10:
3.    Fill_another_bucket(Bucket_of_water)
4.    Bucket_of_water += 1
```

Basically, this program starts with zero buckets of water (the variable, Bucket_of_water), and would run a function (Fill_another_bucket) to retrieve buckets of water over and over again until it has done so ten times, and then it would stop. But, the reality is more like the following piece of code:

Infinite Loop Golem/Broomstick Program

```
1. Bucket_of_water = 0
2. while True:
```

```
3.    Fill_another_bucket(Bucket_of_water)
4.    if Bucket_of_water == Enough_water:
5.        break
6.    else:
7.        Bucket_of_water += 1
```

In this case, the program is supposed to keep running over and over again until it has achieved a point known as "Enough_water." But since that number isn't defined anywhere, this program would simply run over and over again, forever. The reality is that it probably wouldn't run at all, because Python would likely throw an error message up on the screen warning you that you didn't define Enough_water. But, I think we've made our point here. Without defining the limit (or threshold), we end up in this vicious "infinite loop" cycle.

Even if we define an end, real humans worry about other stuff. Maybe there was enough water in the first place and we don't need to get more water. What if the bucket has a hole in it? What if the water is somehow dirty that day? Do we really want that dirty water? A human worker would consider all these things. But a robot, or a program, or a magical broomstick or Golem would not.

In the world of artificial intelligence, we might say that the Golem and the broomstick were not properly "trained" with enough information to understand that they need to stop retrieving water at a certain point. We could call this point a "threshold" or "limit." Or maybe there is some other obstacle or barrier to the task that we haven't thought of ahead of time. We certainly can't preprogram every conceivable thing that might change or go wrong. In everyday life we don't have to, because humans can adapt to new information or new situations as they arise. It would be far better if the Golem or the broomstick were simply "smart" enough to handle all the different variables they might ever encounter. As time goes on, such a smart helper could learn how to overcome these issues and perform the task better and better. That is precisely why A.I. is so important.

Are Plants Smart?

W ell… sort of.
According to some scientists, plants are, in a way, smart. At its most basic level, intelligence can be defined as the ability to solve problems. Plants and other life forms that use photosynthesis to stay alive have been around on Earth for over 850 million years. During that time, they have survived numerous global catastrophes, including volcanoes, asteroids, mass extinctions, ice ages and other massive climate shifts. Somehow, this kingdom of organisms has been able to react to the changing environment around it, over time. Plants have been around on land much longer than animals, and have established themselves on every corner of the Earth. They have evolved the ability to stay dormant over long

periods, develop new chemicals to tolerate extremes in cold and heat, toxins to ward off animals, and different types of leaves to be able to retain water in periods of drought. And, a lot more... In this sense, they seem to be learning how to adapt to new environments, and are remembering old tricks and developing new ones in order to survive. So, one could say that in a sense, plants are smart.

But, is this truly smart behavior? Or, is it simply that plants have, through constant mutation of their DNA and evolution over time, been able to proliferate due in large part to genetic luck? And are they really remembering past climate change experiences, and reacting thoughtfully to new hazards in the world? Probably not. At least, not in the way that we're talking about. Plants surely have genetic memory in their DNA, and can certainly change in response to whatever the planet throws their way. But that's when you take a look at plants as a whole group, not necessarily individual plants. Plants, as a kingdom, have thrived over the years due in large part to a lot of trial and error. A plant by itself, doesn't have the ability to adapt to a new environment so quickly, if at all. Besides, if survival alone were the main measure of intelligence, then single-celled organisms such as bacteria, or half-living particles such as viruses, would be the smartest things around today. The reality is that true intelligence is defined by a lot of different factors aside from just adaptability.

What are the kinds of characteristics that it takes to be "intelligent"?
- Memory
- Communication
- Perception and understanding of the things around you.
- Ability to learn new things.
- Ability to apply existing knowledge to new circumstances, or adapt to new environments.
- Probably more things you can think of...

These capacities define natural animal intelligence, and more specifically, human intelligence. They also define artificial intelligence.

When computer scientists work to create new forms of artificial intelligence, they try their best to design for all of these various elements. But the human brain has taken millions of years to evolve. Developing a completely new form of synthetic intelligence from the ground up is really a gigantic undertaking.

Hominids, which include all the close relatives and ancestors of humans, have only been around for a few million years. Humans (homo sapiens) themselves, have only been around for a very short time in Earth's geologic history. Over the course of the first few hundred million years

Examples of hominids

of brain evolution (including all animals), relatively few major advances have occurred. Certainly, some animals evolved faster senses and even a partial ability to develop tools and communication. For example, dolphins are highly intelligent animals who are not close relatives of humans, evolved in the recent tens of millions of years. (Still, dolphins are not quite as smart as humans—for example, they don't invent new technologies.) It is these recent few million years where the major intellectual moving and shaking has occurred.

Over this time, human brain volumes have changed incredibly quickly—from around 500 cubic centimeters (or cc) in size, to over 1,500 cc. Over three times in size! But, you might ask yourself, what about elephants

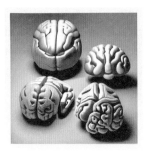

and whales and other large creatures? Don't they also have have huge brains, fantastic memories and abilities to communicate with each other? Shouldn't they be as smart as humans? Indeed, it is true that these large animals have large brains and are pretty smart, but by contrast, some of the largest animals in geological history, the sauropod dinosaurs, had some of the smallest brain to body size ratios in the land-walking animal world. During the same period when our human brains experienced an explosion of growth, our bodies have grown only a tiny bit—staying nearly the same in size. Meaning that, our brain to body size ratios have only been getting bigger and bigger over time, as our intelligence as grown.

On the other hand, if brain to body size ratios were the only measure of intelligence, humans might be just about as smart as mice, since we have very similar ratio of about 1 to 40. Yet we know that are we are far more intelligent than mice. So there must be something else in our heads that makes the difference.

It turns out that in addition to brain volume growth, we have evolved many other fascinating new traits as well. At the cellular level a lot of very exciting changes have taken place. Improvements in our brain cells, otherwise known as neurons, allow them to communicate more quickly and efficiently. This network of neurons is extremely parallel in nature (and we will get into what "parallel" means in an electronic sense, in the next chapter), and very similar to the architecture of modern computer chips. This "neural network" of connections between brain cells is what allows us as humans to become so smart (at least, compared to plants and mice).

When you think about it, it's pretty amazing what humans have been able to accomplish in such a short time. To understand the world around us—from the smallest pieces of matter to the farthest endpoints of the universe. To create civilization, societies, buildings, cities, advanced computer technology and ultimately even create our own new, artificial forms of intelligence. And this neural revolution has all happened in the blink of an eye, compared to the age of the world itself.

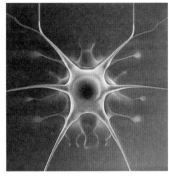

Artistic representation of a neuron

Artificial neural networks are the modern forms of artificial intelligence where some of the most exciting technology is being developed today. These networks are "evolving" much faster than the human brain did. We hope that by the end of this book, you will want to program some of these neural networks. But, before we get into that, we should talk a bit about computer architecture and why it is has proved so difficult to make an artificial man-made system that closely resembles the human brain.

Human Brain vs. Computer

Aspect	Neurons in Human Brain	Transistors in Computer Processors
Basic Unit	Neuron	Transistor
Quantity	Approximately 86 billion	Billions to trillions
Function	Process and transmit information via electrical and chemical signals	Switch and amplify electronic signals
Connectivity	Highly interconnected with synapses (each neuron can connect to thousands of other neurons)	Connected via integrated circuits (containing transistors)
Speed	Milliseconds for signal transmission	Nanoseconds for signal processing
Energy Efficiency	Highly efficient in terms of energy consumption	Less efficient, high power consumption for high-performance tasks
Plasticity	Capable of learning and adaptation (neuroplasticity)	Reprogramming needed for changes
Redundancy	High redundancy; brain can compensate for damaged areas	Lower redundancy; failure of transistors can cause system failures
Operation Mode	Analog and digital processing	Primarily digital processing
Growth and Repair	Can grow new connections and repair to some extent	Cannot self-repair or grow new transistors
Material	Biological cells	Silicon and other semiconductor materials
Data Storage	Distributed across neural networks	Centralized in memory units
Learning Mechanism	Human learning	Machine learning algorithms
Signal Transmission	Chemical synapses, electrical impulses	Electrical signals

Monteith / Get Ready for A.I.

A Brief History of Computers and Their Important Parts

L et's face it—if it weren't for computers, "A.I." would just be "I." And, then how boring would this book be? Computers pretty much define A.I. for what it is, and are the essential tools needed for machine learning to work. As A.I. has become more advanced, the kind and quantity of mathematical computations has become increasingly complex. Computers have had to evolve quickly in order to meet this demand. Outside of A.I., computers have become a major part of our daily lives, in so many ways that we have come to depend on. So, it's important that we talk about them a little bit, and try to understand them better.

Can we all agree that math is hard? Well, at least sometimes it is. Relatively speaking, the kind of math that we learn in elementary and middle school is pretty essential stuff. It's the fundamental math that is used throughout high school and college. At one point or another, we all question why we need to learn this stuff. But as time goes on, it becomes clear that the more complicated math we encounter has roots in what we've learned before. As we encounter new and more complicated types of math, it can feel like a real drag that we often have to do so much simple, basic math, just to get an answer. All that simple math can really slow you down. Not to mention, it's often the simple math that trips you up when solving a bigger equation. That's why so many of us rely on calculators (or smartphones/computers with calculator programs on them) to do this simple math for us. Calculators, or their software equivalents, help to make smaller repetitive math tasks faster, and they help to make sure that our answers are accurate. It is for these reasons, that people have sought to make faster and better counting and calculating machines since some of the earliest days of mathematics.

Counting devices of one kind or another arguably have been around since the days of the abacus, thousands of years ago. But, these low tech devices were manually operated, and had their own limitations. For

one thing, they're not simple to use, and they're only as accurate as the people using them. But still, they represent a major evolution in human thinking about the development of computing devices.

A traditional abacus

Fast-forward to the 20th century, when Bell Labs scientists struck computer gold when they discovered that they could create an "adding machine" using a series of connected automatic switches, known as relays. It wasn't even two years later, that David Packard and Bill Hewlett started a company in their garage that later came to be known as HP, or Hewlett Packard. HP is now famous for printers and laptops, but at that time, in 1939, they were known for audio electronics. In fact, their first product, the HP200A Audio Oscillator, was actually used to create some of the audio for the movie "Fantasia" when it debuted in 1940. In the coming years,

Bell Punch 506D adding machine

more technology innovators jumped into the fray and it was in 1941 that the first true computer, known as the Z3 was created. But it would take several more key innovations in materials to make computer components and their interconnections much smaller. And with smaller size, came more speed— lots of it.

Transistors

Transistors were a key invention in the history of computers. These little guys, still used in computers today, are the places where things get done. Where the 0s and 1s of computer binary happen. In fact, a modern computer chip can have billions of transistors. The first transistors in 1947 were made of germanium and were huge—one of them would fit in your open hand. However, today's transistors are smaller than many molecules. Nowadays, they are under 7 nanometers long—and that's why billions of them can fit onto a single computer chip. A current iPhone has nearly 9 billion transistors in it—and this number is growing all the time.

Early transistors were relatively bulky, made by hand and unreliable. They were also connected to other computer parts by long wires, which were messy and difficult to maintain. Within a decade, a young inventor named Robert Noyce came up with the idea to take all these components and flatten them onto a semiconductor wafer, making them smaller and more efficient. This wafer was made of a material known as silicon (which is where the name "Silicon Valley" comes from.) This was the moment when the integrated circuit was invented. Noyce worked with a colleague named Gordon Moore to perfect this process. Gordon later became famous for his idea known as Moore's Law—the idea that chips will double in transistor density every 18 months. This invention formed the basis of a new company known as Intel, which later became the largest computer chip company in the world, having recently celebrated its 50th anniversary in business. So far, "Moore's Law" has been on track for several decades now, and the amount of transistors has grown exponentially. It is now nearly at the point where the amount of transistors on a chip, or "transistor density" is almost comparable to the amount of neurons in a human brain. And, this is the main reason why true artificial intelligence is now possible.

A circuit board containing integrated circuits - sometimes known as "computer chips"

Memory / Storage

Much like our own human memory, a computer needs to be able to remember things and retrieve those memories quickly in order to get a job done as fast as possible. Computer memory, usually known as RAM, or Random Access Memory, is used by computer chips to take care of short term tasks. In order to be able to run a math function, for instance, a computer might need to remember a string of numbers. So, in order to do more complex calculations, a computer has to remember lots of strings of really long numbers. The more memory a computer has, the easier it is for the computer to get things done. This is why computers used for A.I. often have large amounts of memory in them. A.I., in particular, requires a large amount of calculations, especially when it is learning about something new. Learning new things requires a computer to compare many pieces of data. Sometimes this data can number in the hundreds, thousands or even trillions of individual data points. In cases where the data to be compared is images or videos, these can take up very large amounts of space in a computer. Sometimes, too much. Having a large amount of memory is key to being able to run these calculations smoothly.

In addition to short term memory, computers also need long term memory in order to learn new things. Storage is the term for long term memory that computers use to access pieces of information that don't need to be retrieved quickly. This allows a computer to store the things that it has learned, and to be able to access it later on. Having a fast short term memory, combined with possessing a large amount of long term memory is key to developing greater intelligence.

Microchips / CPUs

A more appropriate name for these chips nowadays is really nanochips. As mentioned above, the size of a single part (such as a transistor) inside these modern chips is measured in nanometers. However, when these chips were first invented in the early 1970's by Intel Engineers Ted Hoff and Federico Faggin, their parts were measured in microns (also known as micrometers). The first microchip, known as the 4004, was $1/8^{th}$ of an inch wide and had only 2,300 transistors in it. A technical marvel of its time. Microchips were the first truly powerful chips that contained all the essential things needed to run a

Rendering of the 4004 chip, with characteristic gold and white colors.

modern computer. They had their own memory, were programmable, can run lots of mathematical calculations and can communicate with a main board (often known as a motherboard) and through that, the outside world. For those of you who love video games, the 4004 also represented the first time a chip was used in gaming; it was the first mainstream processor to be used in pinball games.

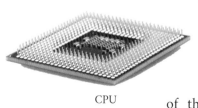

CPU

Microchips have also come to be known as CPUs or Central Processing Units. CPUs are considered the true brains of the computer. All essential computing functions go through these chips, and without them, the computer is nothing!

The IBM "PC"—the first true personal computer—was based on an Intel CPU known as the 8088, just a decade later in the early 1980's. The invention of the microchip, or CPU, brought the world one step closer to personal computers, that would take over the world in more ways than one. Back in these days, computers were still quite expensive, and only governments, large companies and universities could afford them. However, the invention of the CPU and the PC allowed everyday people to be able to afford them. The PC's, combined with core software known as an OS, or Operating System, gave people an affordable and easy-to-operate way of writing their own programs at home. It was around the time that the IBM PC first came out when one of the richest people in the

a PC computer

world, Bill Gates, created Microsoft, and purchased the rights to DOS, which later became Windows. Personal computers with an easy to use OS meant more people could work and collaborate on software, including A.I. software, and ultimately led to the creation of networks and eventually the Internet, which has been such a major part of the growth and success of A.I. around the world.

While early CPUs were not powerful enough to run any significant A.I., modern CPUs such as the Intel i7 and i9 are capable of running A.I. programs at much faster speeds. However, because CPUs are general processors, designed to do many different types of tasks in parallel, they are not necessarily the most efficient processors for running artificial intelligence programs. A new breed of processors has emerged in recent years that has transformed the way A.I. is done.

GPUs, TPUs and more!

The world of specialized chips, or processors, is growing. These special chips are relatively new to the computing scene. Processors with names like GPU, TPU and more, are used for a very specific purpose, unlike CPUs. GPUs are Graphical Processing Units, and are designed specifically to help computers run the graphics you see on monitors much faster. They are better than CPUs for running certain repetitive math functions, and because of this, they're ideal for certain A.I. functions as well. GPUs can really speed up the time that it takes for an A.I. program to learn, or "train" new data. For instance, a data training session that runs on a typical CPU might take 10 hours, but on a GPU, it might only take 10 minutes.

TPUs, or Tensor Processing Units, are specialized chips, similar to GPUs in design, that are used specifically for conducting A.I. functions with a particular program known as Tensorflow, developed by Google. As more and more software developers create chips that work specifically with their A.I. programs, we are seeing A.I. achieve amazing new speeds, and with that, entirely new capabilities. A.I. functions that programmers could not achieve just a few years ago are now achievable, thanks to a combination of technology advances both in software programming as well as hardware like specialized chips.

There is even a new type of A.I. chip being developed in the past couple of years known as a neuromorphic chip. These chips are designed specifically to mimic the human brain, and are ideal for running A.I. programs. In recent times, Intel announced that it scaled its neuromorphic chip system to achieve 100 million "neurons". While a human brain might contain around 100 billion neurons, just think about how far we've come since the 4004—in only a few decades. Computer processors are evolving so quickly, there will surely be groundbreaking new inventions in the coming years that we can barely imagine now. Maybe you will become this new technology's inventor!

Unorganized Machines
- A brief history of A.I.

N ow that we've discussed some of the hardware behind A.I., let's talk a little about how modern A.I. software started out.

Like the history of computing hardware, A.I.'s core math concepts and algorithms started out in the middle of last century. But, unlike many computing inventions, which are usually attributed to individual inventors, the beginnings of artificial intelligence were more of a team effort, built from the contributions of many people working together.

One of the most famous names associated with the history of A.I. is Alan Turing. He was a genius known for

Turing in 1936

his skills both as a mathematician and as an early computer scientist. In fact, the greatest honor in computer science today is named the "Turing Award" after him. He is celebrated for his work in cryptography (making and breaking codes). His work cracking secret Nazi codes with the famed "Enigma Machine" helped the US and its allies win World War II. Turing was also known for his 1948 theory that the human mind, especially that of infants, is an unorganized machine filled with circuits of randomly interconnected axons and

Military Enigma Machine

dendrites (parts of human brain cells known as neurons). Many people feel that this was an early conception of neural networks, which is also how the brain works.

But, perhaps more important than that, in the world of artificial intelligence, is the concept known as the "Turing Test." In this test, considered the one true test of A.I., a human judge holds a virtual conversation with two parties. One is a human, typing answers, and the other is an A.I. machine doing the same. If the human judge, after extensive questioning, is unable to tell the difference between the machine and the other person, then the A.I. machine is said to have "passed the Turing Test." The future day when a machine passes the Turing Test is thought of as a crucial boundary in computer science, not to mention human history. It is the point when computer intelligence will be considered essentially equal

Wartime picture of a Bletchley Park Bombe

to human intelligence—at least as far as its ability to communicate. Many people consider this the goal of most modern work on A.I., and the person or team that achieves this feat is sure to be remembered throughout history.

The actual term "artificial intelligence" didn't arise until just after Turing's death in 1954. Modern artificial intelligence traces its roots to a meeting at Dartmouth College in 1956, called the "Dartmouth Summer Research Project on Artificial Intelligence." This was just a couple years before Robert Noyce (in 1959) patented the silicon integrated circuit, which became the basis of the global semiconductor industry we know today.

A professor named John McCarthy, helped organize the Dartmouth workshop and gave it the name "Artificial Intelligence." Later McCarthy became known as the creator of the A.I. computer language Lisp. Some of the greatest minds involved in the math and computer science behind A.I. at the time attended the workshop. Among them was Marv Minsky, who went on to become the founder of MIT's famous Artificial Intelligence Laboratory.

Old drawing of MIT

At this workshop, many of the core ideas behind modern A.I. were formulated, including natural language processing, the theory of computation, neural networks and more. These ideas formed the basis of some of the very same fields of study that computer scientists focus on today. Natural language processing (NLP), for example, is an area of A.I. dealing with how humans and computers interact using natural forms of communication like spoken language. For instance, when you speak with Apple's Siri phone assistant or Amazon's Alexa devices, the computer uses A.I. to interpret your natural language and then communicates with a program to find the most appropriate data in an online server. Natural language processing is an important technology and one that many people associate with A.I..

While these foundational ideas were important to the future of A.I., it was decades before many of these ideas could succeed. Not everything in engineering history is one big steady, continuous path to success. Most often, there are lots of hiccups, false starts and dead ends. The history of A.I. is a good example of how small mistakes can put a hold on a very promising technology development.

In 1957, Frank Rosenblatt wrote a paper introducing the basic ideas behind the Perceptron. The Perceptron is a type of neural network which conducts "supervised" learning, analyzing one piece of information at a time. This approach contrasts with other types of networks that can analyze multiple pieces of data simultaneously. Supervised learning models like the Perceptron use input data that has been checked and classified by humans already, so that the computer can more easily understand

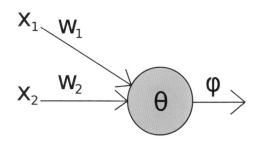

Diagram of a Perceptron

it. Unsupervised learning models, on the other hand, simply read all sorts of data and use multiple layers of analysis in order to learn new things. A great example of a Perceptron at work is something known as OCR (optical character recognition), or alphabetical character and number recognition. This is something many of us use nearly every day when we type things into our smartphones, or scan pieces of paper and convert them into editable word processing documents.

Perceptrons can have one layer or many layers of information connected to each other. When the Perceptron was first conceived and used for the problem of character recognition, it used only one layer. This one-layer system had a very hard time reading certain types of characters. So, it was thought by some people that maybe Perceptrons (aka neural networks) might not be a useful pathway to advance artificial intelligence research. One such person was Marv Minsky—one the "fathers of A.I." himself—who claimed at a number of public conferences that neural networks were probably not going to be very useful. Given his status in the A.I. community, this led to neural networks falling out of favor for a very long time, decades in fact.

However, even though neural networks were out of favor for many years, Rosenblatt stuck with his beliefs that neural network would one day be the predominant algorithm for A.I.. In fact, in a 1958 *New York Times* article he very accurately predicted:

> "Later Perceptrons will be able to recognize people and call out their names and instantly translate speech in one language to speech or writing in another language […]."

> -*New York Times*, "New Navy Device Learns By Doing" 7/7/1958

Based on today's apps, we know that Rosenblatt was right. Minsky, who went on to develop many critical advances in A.I., later admitted that one of his biggest regrets was slowing down the progress of neural network research for so many years.

Over the past half century or so, A.I. would have periods of high research interest and available funding, known as "A.I. Summers." Times when there was less interest and funding for research were known as "A.I. Winters." Well, get your A.I. bathing suit and A.I. flip flops ready, because as time goes on, it is becoming clear that we are entering a very hot summer.

In recent years, neural networks have become incredibly popular, and are now used in much of the A.I.-enabled software all around us. A relatively new neural network approach, known as deep learning, began in 1967, when Alexey Ivachenko wrote a paper about a supervised, deep, multilayer Perceptron. Yet, it wasn't until the late 1980s that the term "deep learning" was coined by Rina Dechter. These systems came into regular use in the 1990s and are commonly used now for a wide number of applications, including speech recognition. Deep learning neural networks include RNNs (Recurrent Neural Networks) and CNNs (Convolutional Neural Networks). Both are in regular use by leading researchers today, and we will discuss them later in more detail.

Over the past few decades, major advances in A.I. have continued to be made by teams of people in government, academic and corporate settings, mainly in computer science departments. But now, more and more people are able to conduct A.I. research in a wider variety of fields, including medicine, energy, agriculture, aerospace and more. While Rosenblatt's Perceptron concept was tested on a $2 million naval research computer, today's average computers, at a fraction of the cost, have far more computing power. Even a basic maker device like a Raspberry Pi is now capable of performing fairly complex computing tasks, including deep learning, for a price tag in the tens of dollars.

Raspberry Pi 2 model B

The rate of A.I. technology development has also increased

substantially with the advent of the Internet and "cloud computing." Even better, there are a great many free, open-source A.I. programs. People around the world are sharing their programs on platforms like github in order to collaborate and build A.I. projects together.

Today, advances in A.I. are often made by people like you and me. And given how powerful the average modern PC is, that means any one of us could invent the system that beats the Turing Test.

A Look at the Basics of Today's A.I.

Some Key Terms & Things To Know

The algorithms and math behind A.I. can be pretty complex stuff. Let's face facts here. It's the kind of math that confuses college graduate students, so it must be pretty hard, right?

Take this value function for instance:

$$v_\pi(s) = \sum_a \pi(a|s) \sum_{s',r} p(s',r|s,a)[r + \gamma v_\pi(s')]$$

Do you have any clue what this does? Neither did I, or anybody I know, at first glance. Something like this is commonly used for what is known as reinforcement learning in A.I.. It takes studying lots of math to really be able to get it, at a deep level. Fortunately, these days you don't need to know all this math to be able to program some meaningful A.I. of your own. Much of the math and the algorithms behind A.I. are now programmed into simple to use functions in open source software like Google's Tensorflow and Keras, and can be programmed using fully open source programming languages, like Python.

Over time, you can learn a lot of this complex math pretty easily, if you break it down into smaller pieces. This becomes easier as you become more familiar with how A.I. works. But, knowledge of the math behind A.I. is no longer an obstacle to creating useful new A.I. applications, or even coming up with your own way of applying existing algorithms. That means people who are less familiar with math and advanced computer science can now apply A.I. to subjects of their own choosing. They may even make discoveries previously overlooked by human eyes and minds.

So, let's talk about some of the most basic concepts that you should be familiar with in A.I.. Boiling it all down to its essence, most modern artificial intelligence is all about picking an appropriate neural network or other core set of algorithms, and using it to train a model with data, so that the system can learn how to understand new, previously unseen information. To put it simply, the process is something like this:

Data —> Neural Network Training —> Model —> Learn/classify/create new things

There are of course a few steps in between, here and there. But, the main thing is to remember that unlike learning about how computers think — in A.I., we're thinking about how computers learn. So, it's important at all times to keep in mind that we're trying to teach computers new ways of learning, like we do as humans. And since A.I. is in its infancy, it's important to remember that we should teach computers as if they too were little babies. We know that infants often make mistakes and do funny things like bang into furniture and cry. They may have a hard time identifying and remembering objects, standing and walking, or doing other things we older people take for granted. Mostly, this is because babies just haven't learned enough about the world yet. That's why they constantly explore, touch everything and are generally so curious about the world. They hunger for more information, more input.

A.I. is quite the same. Only, at the moment, most A.I. is not sophisticated enough to let us know when it requires more data. It just throws an error, or stops working, or simply doesn't work quite right at all. That is why when we design A.I. systems, we need to consider not only the type of data we need, but also how much data we need to get the job done.

In the world of human child development, babies usually crawl, then walk, then talk, in that order. But not always. The time it takes babies to do these tasks varies widely and there can be a huge range of factors that influence this sequence. When babies learn to talk, it is often because their parents (or a digital recording) have been repeating the same words over and over again. This repetition allows the baby to train its mind to recognize certain sounds as words or names. Eventually, after randomly trying numerous sounds on its own, the baby starts to make sounds that get the right response from its parents. The baby is learning how to talk. Machine learning is similar in the sense that the learning rates for different topics or skills can vary widely, and the more input data and the more training the system receives, usually the better it performs.

Most A.I. today is known as narrow A.I., meaning that these A.I. systems are designed for a specific task as opposed to a universal form of A.I. that can handle any general task. For instance, a program that can diagnose COVID-19 patients using chest x-ray data is only trained for that purpose and not trained to recognize speech or play chess. This is one reason why passing the Turing Test is hard, because there is such a large amount of data required to be able to function and communicate as a human.

This book isn't intended to teach you all aspects of A.I., but rather to introduce you to some of the key concepts that make up modern A.I.. Here are some of the terms that you hear about a lot in A.I. these days:

Data

Data is a big topic in A.I.. The data needed for narrow A.I. tasks is usually one type of information. For example, suppose you need to teach an A.I. to find and track a red ball bouncing around a screen among a lot of other colored balls or shapes. In this case you would need to track both shape and color. Since you only need to track one red ball, versus other shapes or balls of other colors, the variety of objects and colors to be recognized is fairly limited. Imagine training a dog to find the red ball in a toy box of other objects. How many times would you have to show the dog? For a computer, the training for this task would not be too difficult. You might have to use as few as hundreds or even dozens of training data points (that is, show the A.I. the red ball in hundreds or dozens of different pictures), depending on the system you are using.

Another example, which is used very commonly in many A.I. texts, is the MNIST database (Modified National Institute of Standards and Technology). The MNIST database is a free set of training data made up of handwritten digits. The database contains 60,000 training data points, along with 10,000 for testing. This is a fairly old dataset, often used for teaching machine learning to students. Using this data, you can train a neural network to understand most handwritten numbers. Since the task of identifying a handwritten number only requires the shape of the figure and doesn't really require color information, this data is offered only in black & white (or grayscale). This makes the input data smaller and more efficient. Because the training data contains a wide variety of characters written by different people, when you train an A.I. model with it, it has a fairly high accuracy in correctly identifying numbers written by new people. Even people with sloppy handwriting!

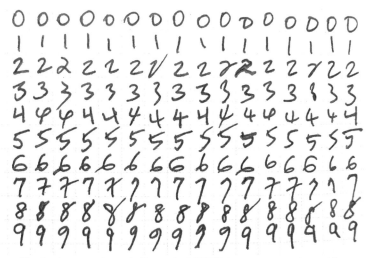

Handwritten numbers, similar to the MNIST dataset commonly used for training educational A.I. models.

But most real-world science A.I. problems are much more difficult. If, for example, you wanted to create a plastic pollution detector to find pieces of plastic on a beach for a science fair project, you might want to train a system that looks at both the shape of the particles as well as their color. That's because plastic particles can be many colors, and can sometimes have shapes that look unique, or look like any rock on the beach. It's a difficult task to create a dataset for this, since the colors and shapes will vary a lot. Even if you built a system good at identifying the colors or specific shapes, it might have a hard time distinguishing clear or white plastic particles on different backgrounds, especially if they look like rocks or seashells. Without a doubt, you would need a large amount of input data, to ensure that the system was properly trained.

There are almost countless possibilities of plastic shapes and colors. In this case, even with a great dataset, with labeled data, and a well-trained model, it would be very hard to make your plastic-identifying A.I. work really well.

An A.I. system's ability to be efficient is highly dependent on its data, and the amount and quality of data that the system uses to learn from. Although as we pointed out above, more data is usually better, it's also best if that data is as tiny and compact as possible.

One of the big things to think about when making data small and efficient is optimizing dimensions. And no, I'm not talking about data from another universe. I mean dimensions as in measurements—like the length, width and height of a bookcase, or X, Y, Z coordinates. X-Y coordinates are 2-dimensional and X-Y-Z coordinates are 3-dimensional, or 3D. Taking a look at the MNIST data, mentioned above, to ensure that the files are as small as possible, the pictures have been reduced to only 28 by 28 pixels, less than 100 bytes of data. By comparison, a really good smartphone camera nowadays is capable of taking pictures of 12MP, which equates to over four thousand pixels just on one side—potentially 10's of megabytes of information. That is a huge difference in data. And, while having higher resolution is generally considered better when we're talking about pictures and monitors and TV screens, when we're talking about A.I. training, having the lowest resolution you can get away with is always best.

There's a lot more information stored in an average digital photograph than you might think. Figuring out the file size of a picture is not simply a matter of mulitiplying out its size dimensions. There's also color information, too. Think of an image. If you are going to turn it into numbers based on color instead of just grayscale, you will need a lot more numbers. Pictures stored as grayscale images are far smaller and more efficient due to the fact that they usually store only 256 different shades of color information in each pixel, ranging from white to black. Color pictures on the other hand are stored as RGB data (meaning Red Blue Green color data) for each pixel. Meaning, color information, representing 256 shades of red, green and blue are stored for every single pixel. Now imagine just how much data that is! This is the main reason why many face recognition systems convert all face data to grayscale images first—to save all those extra bytes of data.

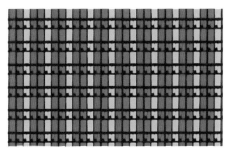

Representation of the tiny RGB pixels on a computer or smartphone screen

Computer Data Units Table

Data Unit	Abbre-viation	Value	Bytes
bit	b	0 or 1	1/8 of a byte
byte	B	8 bits	1 byte
kilobyte	KB	$1,024^{1}$ bytes	1,000 bytes

megabyte	MB	$1,024^2$ bytes	1,000,000 bytes
gigabyte	GB	$1,024^3$ bytes	1,000,000,000 bytes
terabyte	TB	$1,024^4$ bytes	1,000,000,000,000 bytes
petabyte	PB	$1,024^5$ bytes	1,000,000,000,000,000 bytes
exabyte	EB	$1,024^6$ bytes	1,000,000,000,000,000,000 bytes

And of course in these examples, we only discuss image data, but there are many other types of data commonly used in A.I., including sound, biological data, and more. For A.I. to continue to improve the way it has, it's going to need as much efficient data as possible!

Artificial Neural Networks

Neural networks are now known as the main ways to do machine learning. We're going to talk about two of the most well known examples of neural networks—convolutional neural networks, and recurrent neural networks, as well as newer types of networks that have been receiving much attention lately—Generative Adversarial Networks and Transformers.

CNN

Convolutional neural networks. These kinds of neural networks are popular for such machine learning tasks as image recognition. Convolutional neural networks are multi-layer Perceptrons modeled after animal visual cortexes (in their brains). A great example of a CNN is an object detection system, that is capable of identifying specific cards in a deck of playing cards.

RNN

Recurrent neural networks. This type of network is best used for sequential data, like spoken words, stock data, or even music. One example of an RNN is a system that is able to predict the weather based on historical weather sensor data. RNNs are very commonly used in systems that use speech recognition today, and while they are quite fast and efficient, they do have some issues with tasks involving the analysis of longer sequences. One of the ways that computer scientists have tried to fix this is to come up with a specific type of RNN known as LSTM, or Long Short Term Memory, which is commonly used today.

GAN

Generative Adversarial Network. In recent years, these networks have received a considerable amount of attention. Essentially this is a system of two or more neural networks that battle each other, to come up with an output. Most often, this output is a new creation, and that is why the word "generative" is used. GANs are being used today to create some really cool technology that can make completely artificial but highly realistic human faces. Nvidia has created a version of a GAN software recently that produces results so realistic that it is hard to tell the difference between a real person and a GAN generated one. Try it out for yourself: https://www.thispersondoesnotexist.com/

Transformers

Transformers are a type of model in artificial intelligence (A.I.) that are especially good at understanding and generating human language. They work by processing words in a sequence, paying attention to the context and meaning of each word. Imagine reading a sentence and knowing what each word means based on the words around it—that's what transformers do, but with much more data and speed. They are used in many applications, such as translating languages, summarizing texts, and even chatting with you like I am now! One of the most famous transformer models is called GPT, which stands for Generative Pre-trained Transformer.

Models

The goal of most A.I. is to produce a model that has gone through enough training to be able to perform its task—whatever that task may be.

However, we know that producing new models is not only labor intensive but energy intensive too. Training a complex A.I. model can take months and potentially generates as much carbon dioxide as five cars during their entire lifetimes. So, while A.I. does have many potential upsides, one big downside is that computer-intensive training can have a serious impact on the environment. This is why you generally need to be as efficient as possible when creating an A.I. model, to use computer time most effectively, not just to save time and money but to save the atmosphere.

The best way to do that is to start out with a pretty good model that already has been trained with a considerable amount of data in it. There are a number of base models out there that people regularly use for different applications. When choosing a model, you need to consider both speed and accuracy. You might have a model that is known to be 95% accurate in certain applications like recognizing a human body, but it might take a full minute for the data to process. A different model might be only 80% accurate but only take a fraction of

a second. If you were making an A.I. system for a self-driving vehicle, you would have to decide what your priorities were—making sure that you could identify a person with high accuracy, or do it fast enough that you could avoid an accident with a person. In a case like this, you would probably choose speed over accuracy, because you can always require the system to warn you if it saw an object of any kind in the road, whether it was a person or not. On the other hand, if you were using an A.I. image system with a microscope to identify scientific specimens, this certainly wouldn't be a life or death situation. If accuracy were very important, you would probably choose the system with the most accurate identification possible, even if it were very slow. However the ability of all these various models to perform complex functions quickly has been rapidly improving over time.

One of the most well known models in machine learning, ImageNet, was a model based on 14 million images of different objects that have been hand-labeled and classified into 22,000 categories by human curators. It has been used in an annual international competition, to show how accurate deep learning computer vision can be. Year after year, the ImageNet competition has had incredible improvements in terms of accuracy. Winning "nets" then were quickly incorporated into deep learning systems around the world.

Weights, Biases & Activation Functions

If there is one section in the book that is likely to cause your brain to explode, this is the one. So we'll do our best to keep it short and to the point.

Weights, biases and activation functions are the things that a machine learning system actually uses to learn something. They're probably the most important things in neural networks, but they're also some of the most confusing. And, from a math formula point of view, weights and biases go hand in hand with each other. Weights decide how much emphasis to put on an input when analyzing data for the model. This is very important because imagine if you were writing a program for basic human face recognition—a program whose only job is to find people in a photograph. Is there one feature that you would weigh more heavily, or weigh less? Humans tend to have the same basic features as other animals, like noses, eyes, ears, mouths, etc.. But maybe human eyebrows and hair are more pronounced. So, perhaps you would put more "weight" on those? But what about people who have short hair or no hair? Deciding on the weights in applications even as simple as basic face recognition can be quite tricky.

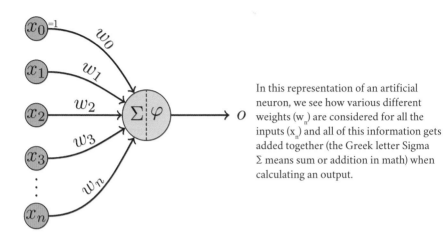

In this representation of an artificial neuron, we see how various different weights (w_n) are considered for all the inputs (x_n) and all of this information gets added together (the Greek letter Sigma Σ means sum or addition in math) when calculating an output.

While a bias might sound like negative word, when we're talking about human thinking about each other, bias in neural network formulas is quite the opposite. In fact, bias in A.I. is a constant; it doesn't change, and it simply gets added to the analysis, to make sure that each neuron in the network can pass data to other neurons. Bias ensures continuity—that a model can keep learning new things after it has already learned other things.

Now, there is also a concern that human bias and data bias does affect A.I.. For instance, in face recognition systems, do the algorithms work better with white faces, rather than faces of color? This is a major concern today that bias in A.I. is already a big problem and if nobody does anything about it, it will continue to grow and become a bigger problem. A.I. should, of course, be treating everybody equally. In addition, bias in data happens, when small problems in a dataset (usually due to problems in the training data) can cause a machine learning system not to work correctly. Bias in the human sense is something we will address later on.

$$Y = \sum (\text{weight} * \text{input}) + \text{bias}$$

Here is another way of looking at this. In neural networks, we use mathematical functions (activation functions) that take all the relevant weights and biases into consideration, to come up with an output. In this case, the output of this artificial neuron is Y.

A detailed mathematical explanation of activation functions is beyond the scope of this book, but let's just say that activation functions are the mathematical equivalents of the firing of neurons that occurs within your brain. The reason for the need to create a mathematical equivalent of the function is to try and emulate the workings of the human mind as closely as possible. The best example for the development of an artificial neural network is most certainly a biological one, and while not perfect, activation functions serve the function of allowing calculations to continue to be passed from neuron to neuron without stopping. The longer that an artificial neural network can "think" about something, the more likely it is to come up with its own conclusions and learn something.

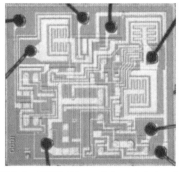

This is a "555" chip, an integrated circuit capable of performing tasks related to timing. An integrated circuit can be seen as a network of physical components resembling functions that turn ON/1 or OFF/0, depending on variable input, not very different from the firing of a neuron.

Training

Training is essentially learning. A neural network needs to be able to understand new things, and it can only do so if it has experienced similar things in the past. As in human learning, A.I. can always continue to learn, without ever stopping. Experts in languages can never truly learn every word or every piece of literature. Piano virtuosos can keep practicing their whole lives and not be able to master every composition ever written. Even geniuses across multiple fields have no reason to stop learning new things, since there is always more to learn.

Training an A.I. system is similar in the sense that, you can always keep training it more and more (well, in actuality, you can indeed train A.I. too much, but usually more training is better). However the question is, if you want to use that A.I. system for something practical, then at some point, you simply need to pause the training and put the trained model into action. Unlike human learning, a lot of basic A.I. programs today are unable to effectively learn at the same time that they train. Computer scientists are working on that problem now. So, it is important to know when your system has "learned enough" to carry out the job it was designed to do. This can be tricky, and we talk about this in the next chapter.

In general, more training with more data does usually yield better results in A.I.—but not always.

Inference

After you've trained a model with your own data, it's time to deploy. Once you have created a specifically trained model that you feel has enough built-in "knowledge" to begin performing its task, you can re-publish your model in a compact version known as an inference graph. This is essentially a new model, modified by your own training, that does something specific.

Data Augmentation

Data Augmentation is basically fake data. It's one of those odd things in computer science, because it's really what every teacher tells you NOT to do—and that is to make up the results. But, unlike in school, you won't get in trouble for using data augmentation in A.I.. It's actually quite a necessary thing, as model training requires such a large amount of data, that in some cases you simply just can't find enough. So you need to make it up. Sometimes it can be as simple as taking image files, and reversing them or rotating them a bit, like in the below example with puppy dog data. But, in other cases, you need to use A.I. to create all new, entirely fake data to supplement your real data.

Data augmentation helps to enlarge the amount of your training data, by simply creating some variations of the input data (in this case, a puppy in different orientations).

Visualizing A.I.
- Diagrams, Charts & Other Stuff

O n the surface, A.I. can seem like a pretty complicated thing. Take for instance this diagram of a neural network:

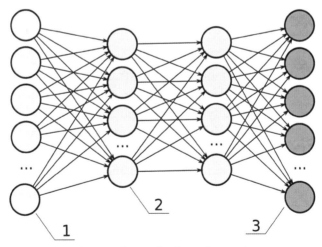

A diagram of an artificial neural network

One of the main reasons A.I. can seem like a scary subject to study is because of all these complicated diagrams and graphs. But the reality is, to get started, we really don't need all these hard-to-read math equations and formulas. A lot of A.I. can be boiled down to a few basic concepts, which don't require much jargon or too many complex charts to understand. Let's talk about a few examples of core A.I. concepts and how to understand the graphs that are associated with them.

We all know that as babies, when we learn things, we do so with both positive reinforcement, and negative reinforcement. Or another way people say this is with "carrots and sticks." What we mean by this, is that often we learn how to walk when we can achieve the goal of reaching our destination (a "carrot") and we can also learn how to walk by not falling on the ground or slamming into walls (a "stick"). In a sense, all of this positive and negative reinforcement serves a way of "training" our minds the next time we encounter a similar situation. A.I. learns in similar ways. It learns both when it correctly identifies the right information, but it also learns and improves overall when it is able to correctly figure out what the wrong answer or approach would be as well. There are a lot of wrong answers out there, that can seem right. In many cases, there are more wrong answers than right answers. And that's why having the proper training, and the ideal amount of training, is critical in A.I..

As a typical A.I. model is being trained, it is constantly processing training data, while checking the results of the model against a set of testing data. For a typical A.I. application like object detection (when you use, say, a webcam to identify a specific object like a baseball among other random objects), it is typical to collect a large amount of images as input data. Then, after using special software to label images in such a way that the computer can identify the target objects, you divide the files into two categories: training and testing. This is done so that the A.I. program can check its own progress. It's typical to use a ratio of 70-80% training data to 20-30% testing data, or something in that ballpark. As model training progresses, the results of this testing process are usually logged, in the form of positive correct identifications (accuracy/precision) as well as negative/incorrect answers (loss).

One simple-looking, yet sort of complicated graph you might encounter when training your own A.I. is known as the "loss curve." This curve helps you learn information about the progress of data training in A.I., to better understand when the model is finished, or when it's close enough to being fully trained. At least, trained enough to perform its intended job.

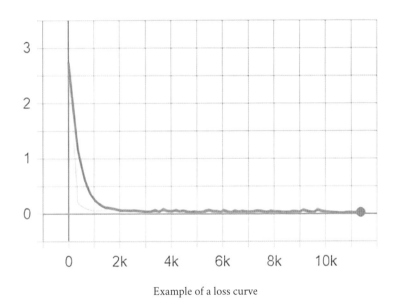

Example of a loss curve

The loss curve is essentially a way to show how many times the model tests itself, and gets a wrong answer. It is useful to data scientists because once the line goes completely flat, and the closer it is to 0, then that means your model is pretty much trained. Training any further won't yield any better results, and might even potentially ruin the model.

Accuracy (or precision), is just the opposite. When you look at a graph showing the accuracy of a model, compared to the loss, it almost looks like some sort of mirror. This means that accuracy is the inverse of, or the opposite of, loss. That's because as the system checks itself and it starts to get more and more correct answers, it also gets fewer wrong answers. Eventually, both the loss and the accuracy reach a stable, flat plateau, at which point the system can't get too many more right or wrong answers.

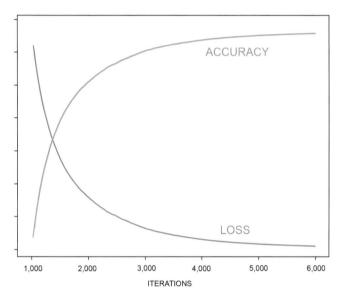

Accuracy vs. loss; note how these two curves seem to be the opposite of each other; this is also known as an "inverse correlation"

It is important to be able to know when a system is trained sufficiently, because as we mentioned before, it can take a really long time to train some models. It can be not only very time-consuming but it is also very wasteful of resources. It was once calculated that some large scale A.I. models can emit more carbon into the atmosphere than 5 cars during their lifetimes. That's because all that computing power uses electricity, which often comes from fossil fuel sources. It's important to make sure we don't destroy the environment just for the sake of some A.I. models. That's why more computer scientists are looking at the new idea called TinyML (tiny machine learning), which is a concept that strives to make A.I. models and training smaller, more efficient and mostly important, cause less impact on the environment.

This also lends itself to a new trend in A.I. known as AIOT, which is sort of a combination of A.I. and the Internet of Things (IOT). As people begin to use smaller, more complicated, and in some cases Internet-connected electronic devices in their everyday lives, this opens up the possibility of using A.I. in more ways, everyday. Imagine a world with small A.I.-enabled devices all around us, helping us out throughout our regular tasks.

Once you have a trained model, whether it's "tiny" or humongous, then it's time to deploy it. And that means, put it to work in the real world. Every A.I. model is different, and is built for specific goals in mind. So, let's talk about a common example. Let's say you're building an A.I. model to do object classification. Specifically, to do specimen classification for something you like to collect. Maybe, you want your A.I. model to use a webcam to review and classify your fossil collection. And, you'd like to classify a few basic invertebrate fossil types. Say, fish fossils, brachiopods (which are like seashells), crinoids (which look a little bit like flowers) and trilobites (which were the first animals to develop vision).

Now if we were classifying tennis balls vs fossils, that might be an easy task. Because one thing is bright green and the fossils are different shades of grey and brown. Not to mention, a ball is a round and uniform shape, while fossils can be lots of sizes and shapes. Some fossils might be broken, some might be tiny and others might be crushed or otherwise misshaped from millions of years of being underground. So, to A.I., this might just be a pretty hard problem.

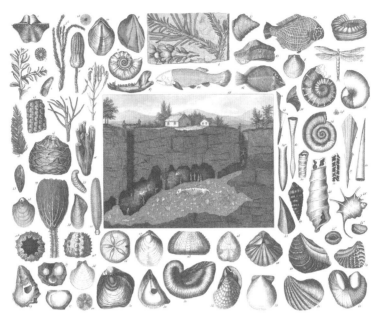

An old illustration of various seashells/fossil specimens

One of the other issues here is that, to an A.I. program, some of these creatures can seem pretty similar to each other. So, when we deploy our model, how can we know that it will identify the right objects? How can we know that it will identify any objects at all?

Here's where another key aspect of A.I. comes in—thresholding. A threshold, you may have heard, is what the groom needs to carry a bride over, after their wedding, according to old traditions. It's a strip of wood, metal, or stone forming the bottom of a doorway and crossed in entering a house or room. In a similar sense, in A.I. it's also a data boundary.

A.I. object detection, showing very high accuracy identification of a fossil ammonite and trilobite

In object detection A.I., it's often the boundary between a correct identification and an incorrect identification of something. In A.I., we set thresholds to determine the cut off line for what we consider a proper identification of something. Often a good threshold is determined by trial and error, after trying out the model in the real world.

If the threshold is set too low, we will end up with a lot of identifications that are just not correct. In the case of our fossil example, if we set the threshold very low, in order to try and identify as many fossils as possible, we might end up with mostly identifications that aren't even fossils. On the other hand, if the thresholds are set too high, we may not be able to identify anything useful at all.

For the system to be practical, the model has to be accurate enough to make the proper identifications, and the thresholds have to be adjusted for each situation that might be encountered.

In a real world scenario, the fossils might be jumbled together in a pile right next to each other, or they might be far apart from each other, and easy to spot. In either case, there are benefits and drawbacks to setting the threshold high or low. Depending on how much "background noise" there is, or other objects that can confuse the system, and whether or not the model was trained with a large enough set of different types, sizes and shapes of the fossils. So, there isn't one single answer or formula to determine the right threshold—there are lots of other factors to consider. That's why some people say that A.I. isn't an exact science. It's a combination of math, science, engineering and knowledge about lots of other subjects—and making it all work just right can actually be a little bit like magic.

Correlation

But not all A.I. is about images. In the case of music, climate/weather or financial markets, we would take a look at numerical data from a string of notes or different types of weather sensors, or daily stock prices. We would then use the past history of the sequence of numbers as our training data, along with a small amount of test data, and then create a model that is able to predict a future set of numbers.

In the case of something like a prediction of sea level rise over time due to climate change, it's fairly safe to say that we can see a pattern here, which we could probably predict fairly far into the future—perhaps even decades. Based on what we know about the correlation between climate change and sea levels (over these 140+ years of data), we would say there is a high confidence, or probability, that we could predict this line would continue to rise. And, it would probably rise with a similar looking curve well into the future. That is, unless humans make major changes and do something to stop global warming, right away.

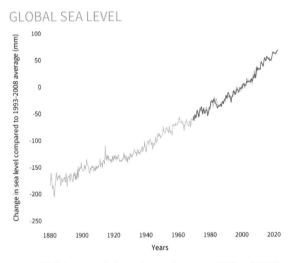

Global sea level rise estimates between 1880 and 2021

And, for an example of sequential financial data, let's take a look at this chart of the S&P500. In the stock market, this is known as an index. It's a way of tracking the average stock performance of 500 of the top companies in the US. Note that over time it tends to go up, but not in a perfectly straight line. There are some times when

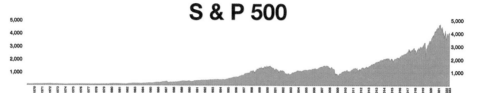

it goes up faster than others. Occasionally it goes down. Something like this would be very difficult to predict for a few weeks, or even a few days. Often it is difficult to predict what will happen from one minute to the next. However, if you had another string of sequential data to compare to, like another stock market index, then you'd have something to compare to. You might even be able to use one index to predict another. For instance, if we compare the S&P Index to the Dow Index, you can begin to see a pattern.

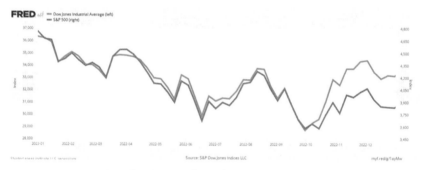

2022 Dow Jones Industrial Average and S&P 500

We would say that these two graphs are highly correlated. So, if you knew that the Dow Index (also known as the Dow Jones Industrial Average) was going to go up, you would then be able to predict that the S&P 500 would go up as well. When you see these patterns, or correlations, you can begin to make meaningful connections between the data, and accurate predictions. You might find making a useful prediction extremely difficult if you had nothing to correlate to (like the S&P 500 stock price graph above). But if you had some other data that you could correlate, then it might be easier to create a set of data that could be useful in creating an A.I. model. This A.I. model, with various correlated training data, could then be used to make predictions. For instance, you could correlate Google trends keyword data (things that people are searching for online) to stock prices, to see what stocks will be "hot" or active today based on whatever is popular at the moment. And maybe you could even use that A.I. model to become a billionaire (or if your model isn't quite perfect, you could lose everything!) Correlations can be made with a wide variety of different types of data—and some are quite difficult to model. For instance, music and voices are relatively difficult tasks for modern A.I, but things are really improving quickly.

This is a visual of sheet music, which many of us are familiar with:

It's an effective way to take a look at sound (music) data that has been around for a very long time.

Here is a spectrogram of some music (a way of representing sounds as a colorful graph):

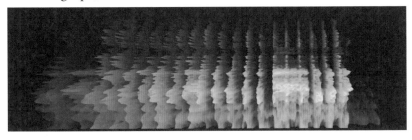

This is how music looks, when it is generated as an MP3 file, like you might play on your smartphone or iPod:

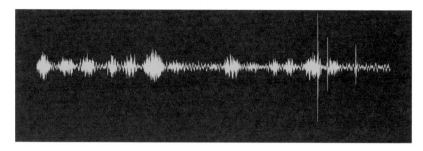

And here is a midi file, which has been commonly used in musical A.I. training, but doesn't have quite the same depth of sound as an MP3 file above:

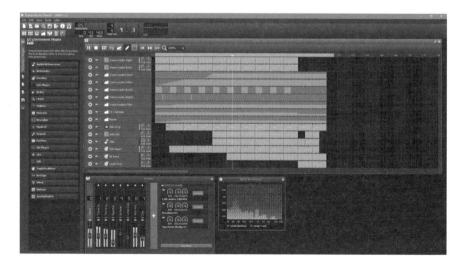

In this case, the midi file shows a portion of a song, and the various instruments that come together to make this song (the green and purple bars). For a bit of a change from the electronic world, here is something biological. It's an electrocardiogram, or ECG chart. Using this data,

A.I. experts and data scientists are now able to determine if someone is having a heart attack, and with a relatively high degree of accuracy, be able to predict a heart attack that is about to happen:

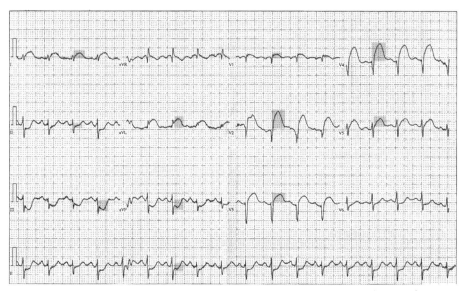

This is ECG (electrocardiogram) data showing the beating of a human heart; in this case, there are indications that this patient may have a potential heart problem.

All of these represent just a small fraction of different data types that are commonly used in sequential data analysis (also sometimes known as time-series data). Cameras, microphones, sensors of all kinds, and other forms of computer-interfaced input all make data that can be visualized in different ways, and used to make next generation A.I. applications.

There is a world of information out there, that could be used in A.I. programs, and we've only just begun to scratch the surface in terms of what we can do with it.

Real World
A.I. Applications

$A.I.$'s applications are vast and constantly evolving. We've touched on a few real world examples throughout the book, but here are some of the most promising areas where A.I. is making a significant impact, that could be part of your future career. Or at least a part of your next science fair project:

Healthcare

A.I. is like a super-powered medical assistant that can crunch massive amounts of health data to spot patterns and predict health problems way before they become serious. It's like having a doctor with a built-in crystal ball!

Here's how it works: Imagine doctors feeding mountains of information about patients—stuff like X-rays, blood tests, and treatment records—into a giant computer brain. This A.I. brain can then analyze all that data lightning fast, looking for hidden clues. These clues can help doctors:

Catch diseases earlier: A.I. can spot tiny changes in scans or blood work that might be too subtle for even the sharpest human eye. This means catching things like cancer or heart trouble in their early stages, when they're much easier to treat.

Craft personalized treatment plans: Imagine having a treatment plan designed just for you, taking into account your age, lifestyle, and even your genes! A.I. can help doctors create these customized plans by analyzing how similar patients responded to different treatments in the past.

Develop new life-saving drugs: A.I. can analyze mountains of scientific data to find promising new drug targets. It's like having a super-powered chemist that can sift through millions of possibilities to find the perfect recipe for a new medicine.

So, the next time you visit the doctor, there might be a silent A.I. partner in the room, working tirelessly behind the scenes to keep you healthy!

Climate Change and Sustainability

Picture this: what if we had a super-smart tool that could analyze everything from air and ocean temperatures to ice core data and satellite imagery, painting a complete picture of Earth's climate system? That's exactly what A.I. is becoming for our planet. By crunching massive amounts of climate data at lightning speed, A.I. can predict weather patterns with much greater accuracy. This isn't just about knowing if tomorrow will be sunny or rainy—it's about predicting extreme weather events like hurricanes and droughts months, or even years, in advance. With this kind of foresight, communities can prepare evacuation plans, stockpile resources, and take steps to minimize damage. But A.I.'s role goes way beyond weather forecasting. Imagine having a tireless environmental detective constantly monitoring air and water quality, deforestation rates, and even tracking the health of our oceans. By analyzing this data, A.I. can pinpoint areas with high pollution levels or identify regions at risk of rising sea levels. This information is crucial for governments and organizations to make informed decisions about environmental protection strategies. Furthermore, A.I. can become a champion for renewable energy. By analyzing historical weather patterns and energy consumption data, A.I. can help optimize the placement and operation of solar and wind farms, maximizing their efficiency and minimizing reliance on fossil fuels. So, next time you hear about climate change, remember there's a whole team of A.I. scientists working behind the scenes. They're using their smarts to fight for a healthier planet for all of us, by providing the insights and predictions needed to make a real difference.

Transportation

Buckle up for a ride into the future of transportation! Imagine cars that can drive themselves, using super-smart A.I. as their brain and brawn. These A.I. algorithms are like expert navigators, constantly analyzing the ever-changing traffic flow around them. They can take in information like the number of cars on the road, the speed everyone's traveling at, and even things like upcoming construction zones or sudden downpours. By crunching all this data in real-time, self-driving cars can chart the safest and most efficient course possible. This means smoother rides, less stop-and-go traffic jams, and a significant reduction in accidents caused by human error—which is a major cause of road woes today.

Imagine a world where traffic lights can communicate with self-driving cars, creating a wave of synchronized movement that keeps everything flowing freely. With A.I. at the wheel, our roads could become safer for everyone, from drivers and passengers to pedestrians and cyclists. It's like having a guardian angel in the driver's seat, constantly looking out for everyone's safety and making sure we all reach our destinations quickly and smoothly.

Education

Imagine ditching the one-size-fits-all approach to learning and instead having a super-smart tutor customized just for you! That's the potential of A.I.-powered tutoring systems. These systems are like brainiac study buddies that can analyze your strengths and weaknesses in any subject. They do this by keeping tabs on your performance, like the answers you give and the mistakes you make. Based on this data, the A.I.  tutor can create a personalized learning plan just for you. Struggling with a specific concept in math? The A.I. tutor will cook up a batch of practice problems that target that exact weakness, along with clear explanations tailored to your learning style. Need a refresher on a history topic? It can whip up interactive quizzes and simulations that make learning feel like playing a game. A.I. can even become a virtual classmate, engaging you in discussions and debates on the topic, helping you solidify your understanding. So next time you hit a snag in your studies, remember there might be a future where A.I. tutors are there to give you that personalized push you need to succeed.

Robotics

Get ready for a future filled with super-powered robots that can think and act alongside us! A.I. is the secret sauce that's taking robots from clunky machines to amazing helpers. Imagine robots outfitted with this super-intelligence, tackling jobs that are dangerous or just plain difficult for humans.

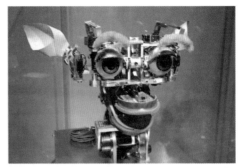

Kismet, a robot developed at MIT that is capable of emulating human emotions.

These A.I.-powered robots could be sent into hazardous environments like burning buildings or radioactive waste sites, fearlessly working to keep people safe. But that's not all. In hospitals, A.I. robots could become a surgeon's right-hand bot, assisting in delicate operations with incredible precision and steady movements. Imagine a tiny robot with super-human dexterity, holding tiny instruments and helping surgeons perform minimally invasive procedures. Even outside of these high-pressure situations, A.I. robots have the potential to become our companions. They could be there for the elderly, providing assistance with daily tasks and offering friendly conversation to keep them company. As A.I. continues to develop, these robots will become even more sophisticated, able to learn, adapt, and perform a mind-boggling range of tasks. The future of robotics is bright, and A.I. is the key that will unlock a world of possibilities where robots work alongside us to make our lives safer, healthier, and more fulfilling.

Cybersecurity

Picture this: an army of digital bodyguards constantly scanning your computer network, looking for sneaky intruders. That's what A.I. cybersecurity systems are like! These systems are whizzes at analyzing massive amounts of data, like network traffic and user activity. They can spot suspicious patterns in real-time, like unusual login attempts or sudden spikes in data downloads. Imagine A.I. noticing someone trying to access your files from a strange location in the middle of the night—a red flag for any security system. The A.I. can then spring into action, blocking the access and alerting you or your IT team to the potential threat. But A.I. isn't just a digital watchdog; it's also a master strategist. By analyzing past cyberattacks, A.I. systems can learn to  predict new hacking techniques and identify vulnerabilities in your network before they're exploited. It's like having a security system that can adapt and evolve alongside the ever-changing tactics of cybercriminals. As cyber threats become more complex, A.I. will play a vital role in keeping our data safe. These A.I. defenders will be on the front lines, working tirelessly to protect our information and keep our digital world secure.

A.I.'s Coolest Technologies

Dive into the Cutting Edge

Forget clunky robots and emotionless machines—A.I. is on the rise, and it's packing some serious superpowers! As we started to mention earlier in the book, one of the hottest areas is Artificial Neural Networks (ANNs) like CNNs, RNNs or Transformers. Think of them like a super-brainy web inspired by the connections in our brains. These networks can process massive amounts of data, constantly learning and adapting—just like how plants adjust to their environment. They even have a kind of memory, storing information from past experiences.

But hold on, A.I. isn't quite human-level intelligent yet. True intelligence involves a whole toolbox of skills—memory, communication, problem-solving, and more. Our brains, with their complex structures and lightning-fast connections, are the gold standard. While ANNs mimic some of these connections, they don't capture the full picture.

This quest to build a brain-like A.I. is mind-blowing. Think about how human brains have evolved for millions of years, allowing us to explore space, build cities, and invent amazing tech! A.I. is still young, but its potential is staggering.

Now, let's zoom in on some specific A.I. technologies that are changing the game:

Talking Like a Human with Natural Language Processing (NLP): Enter ChatGPT, the Superstar of A.I. Chat

Imagine a future where chatbots aren't just frustrating automated menus, but engaging conversation partners who understand your jokes, follow complex arguments, and even adapt their tone to match yours. That future is closer than you think, thanks to the incredible advancements in Natural Language Processing (NLP) and the rise of superstars like ChatGPT, a cutting-edge language model.

Think back to the chatbots you may have encountered before. They might have understood simple questions like "What's the weather like today?" but struggle with anything more complicated. ChatGPTs are game-changers in this arena. These A.I. whizzes are trained on massive amounts of text data, allowing them to process information and respond in surprisingly realistic ways. They can write different kinds of creative text formats, from poems to computer code, and even translate languages with impressive accuracy. But what truly sets them apart is their ability to hold conversations that feel natural.

Here's why ChatGPTs are the Michael Jordan of A.I. chat:

Supercharged Speed: ChatGPTs process information at lightning speed, responding to your questions and requests in milliseconds. Imagine having a conversation where the other person keeps up with your train of thought, no awkward pauses or lagging responses.

Understanding Your Nuances: ChatGPTs aren't just about spitting out pre-programmed responses. They can analyze the context of your conversation, including sarcasm, humor, and even cultural references. This means you can have a natural back-and-forth, where the A.I. understands the real meaning behind your words.

Learning on the Fly: Think of ChatGPTs as language sponges, constantly absorbing new information and adapting their responses. The more you interact with them, the better they get at understanding your preferences and personal style of communication.

The potential applications of ChatGPTs are mind-boggling. Here are a few glimpses into the future:

Personalized Education: Imagine a tutor that tailors its explanations to your specific learning style. ChatGPTs could analyze your strengths and weaknesses, then adjust their teaching approach to help you grasp even the most complex concepts.

Revolutionizing Customer Service: ChatGPT powered chatbots could understand your concerns and offer personalized solutions, making customer service interactions faster, smoother, and even friendly.

Breaking Down Language Barriers: Imagine a world where language is no longer a barrier to communication. ChatGPTs could translate conversations in real-time, fostering collaboration and understanding across cultures.

The Future of Creative Writing: Writers, rejoice! ChatGPTs could become your ultimate brainstorming partner. Stuck on a story plot point? Need help crafting the perfect dialogue for a play? These A.I. can analyze your existing work and suggest creative solutions, helping you take your writing to the next level.

The future of communication is changing rapidly, and ChatGPTs are at the forefront of this revolution. As A.I. continues to evolve, the lines between human and machine conversation will continue to blur. The possibilities are endless, and the future of language is looking more exciting—and interactive—than ever before.

Boom! You're an A.I. Artist: The Magic of Generative Image Creation

Imagine creating mind-blowing images with just a few clicks or a quick voice command—no paintbrushes, easels, or messy studios required! That's the power of generative image creation, a cutting-edge technology that's putting the power of art in everyone's hands.

Think of it as having a super-powered computer program that can turn your wildest ideas into reality. Want to see a photorealistic image of your dog surfing a giant wave on Mars? Or maybe you'd love to create a trippy masterpiece inspired by your favorite video game? Generative image creation tools, like Stable Diffusion, can make it happen!

These A.I. wizards work their magic by analyzing massive amounts of data, learning from real-world images and artwork. They use this knowledge to not just copy existing pictures, but to actually create something brand new based on your input.

Here's how generative image creation is transforming the world:

Concept Art Blast-Off! Struggling to visualize that epic scene for your comic book or video game? Generative image creation tools can help! Sketch out a basic idea, feed it into the program, and watch as your characters and environments come to life in stunning detail.

Fashion Design on Fast Forward: Imagine

brainstorming new clothing lines in seconds! Generative image creation can take your initial sketches and create variations with different patterns, colors, and styles. This lets fashion designers explore tons of ideas quickly and easily.

Special Effects Spectacle: Movies and video games are getting even more mind-blowing with the help of generative image creation. These tools can create realistic-looking creatures, futuristic landscapes, and other special effects that would have taken forever (and a ton of money) to create traditionally.

Keep in mind, because A.I. can now create completely fake visuals that seem very real, it's important to use generative image creation tools responsibly and ethically. But one thing is for sure—the future of art is looking bright, and generative image creation is putting the power to create amazing visuals in the hands of everyone, from professional artists to you!

Game On, Get Smart: How A.I. Learns Through Play

Remember that time you spent hours mastering a new video game? You weren't just having fun (well, hopefully!), you were also learning and getting better at the game. Now, imagine using this same idea to train robots and other A.I. systems! That's the magic of reinforcement learning (RL), a technology where A.I. learns by playing games and facing challenges.

Think of RL as a super-powered training program that uses games to teach A.I. systems new skills. The A.I. plays the game over and over, trying different strategies and learning from its mistakes. Just like you learned to dodge enemies and level up in your favorite game, RL systems get better at whatever task they're tackling with each attempt.

This might sound like fun and games (pun intended!), but RL has serious applications that could change the world! Here are a few examples:

Robot Revolution: Imagine robots that can learn to perform complex tasks, like surgery or assembling furniture, just by playing specially designed games! RL can help robots adapt to different situations and make better decisions in the real world.

A.I. Masters of the Game: Want to see an A.I. beat you at your favorite video game? Well, with RL, that future might not be far off! RL can train A.I. systems to become masters of complex games, even games with constantly changing rules or unpredictable opponents. This can help us develop better A.I. for things like strategy games or even self-driving cars.

Unveiling the Mysteries of Medicine: Scientists are using RL to tackle huge challenges in medicine, like understanding how proteins work. AlphaFold, an A.I. system powered by RL, can predict protein structures with incredible accuracy. This is a game-changer for drug discovery, as understanding protein structures is crucial for designing new medications.

RL is opening up exciting new possibilities for A.I., and it's all thanks to the power of learning through play! So, the next time you're crushing a level on your phone, remember, you might be helping to train the future of A.I.!

A 3D visual of a protein, similar to those produced by AlphaFold.

See the World Like a Computer: The Power of A.I. Vision

Imagine your phone being able to "see" the world around you almost as well as you can! That's the magic of computer vision, a branch of A.I. that's teaching machines to truly see and understand their surroundings. And at the heart of this revolution are Convolutional Neural Networks (CNNs), the brainiacs behind this incredible technology.

Think of CNNs as super-powered image analysis tools. They're trained on massive amounts of pictures and videos, learning to recognize objects, faces, and even movements with impressive accuracy. This lets them do amazing things, like:

Self-Driving Superstars: Ever wondered how self-driving cars navigate busy streets? CNNs play a huge role! They analyze images from cameras in real-time, helping cars identify pedestrians, traffic lights, and other objects on the road. This allows them to make safe decisions and avoid accidents.

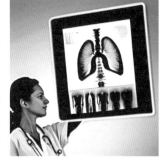

X-Ray Vision for Doctors: Doctors are getting a helping hand from CNNs in the form of smarter medical imaging tools. These A.I. systems can analyze X-rays, MRIs, and other scans, highlighting potential problems and even suggesting diagnoses. This can lead to faster, more accurate medical care.

Security Systems with Super Sight: Keeping you safe just got a high-tech upgrade! Security cameras powered by CNNs can now identify suspicious activity, recognize faces, and even track objects in real-time. This helps security personnel respond to threats quickly and efficiently.

CNNs are also helping us see the world in new ways, and that's opening doors to a future filled with exciting innovations. Imagine using your phone to identify a rare bird in the park or translate a foreign language sign just by pointing your camera at it! The possibilities are endless. But bear in mind, ensuring responsible use of A.I. vision and protecting people's privacy is important.

The future of A.I. is a fusion of these powerful technologies. Now, imagine a world where self-driving cars use a combination of A.I. techniques to navigate smoothly and safely. Or picture medical robots that leverage different A.I. tools to perform delicate surgeries or assist doctors in complex procedures. These advancements are just the beginning—A.I. has the potential to transform industries, boost human capabilities, and reshape our world in ways we can only begin to imagine.

So, the next time you see a cool A.I. application, remember, it's not magic—it's the power of cutting-edge technology pushing the boundaries of what's possible. And who knows, maybe you'll be the one using these amazing tools to create the future!

A.I. of the Future

E ver wondered what artificial intelligence (A.I.) might look like way, way into the future? Well, based on how fast today's A.I. is advancing, let's imagine where this could go. Let's think of a world where A.I. is like having a super-smart buddy who can do almost anything you can think of, but way cooler.

It will be very likely that these A.I. buddies are not just smart but also incredibly helpful. They're not just in our phones or computers; they're everywhere! These A.I. pals might help us do everyday stuff like cooking, cleaning, and homework, but they'll also help us do the big things like finding cures for diseases, exploring space, and even solving big global problems like climate change.

In this future, A.I. won't just understand language; it will truly understand emotions. They'll know how to cheer us up when we're sad, celebrate with us when we're happy, and even offer advice when we're confused. Imagine having an A.I. friend who knows you so well that it can anticipate what you need even before you ask!

But wait, there's more! These future A.I.s might be part of our daily lives in ways we can't even imagine now. They could be in our clothes, helping us stay healthy and fit, or in our bicycles, making sure we're always safe on the road. Some people think that in the not-too-distant future, we will have A.I. assistants everywhere, who can be creative like humans—helping to make art, music, and stories that touch our hearts. These assistants might become so creative that they'll invent new things that we've never even dreamed of before!

These advanced A.I. friends will also be super ethical and fair. They'll make decisions that are not just smart but also right for everyone. They'll help us build a world where everyone has a fair chance and where nobody is left behind.

But remember, while these future A.I.s might be super helpful and smart, they'll still need us. They'll need our guidance and kindness to make sure they're using their powers for good and helping humanity grow and thrive.

And you know what's even cooler? You might be the ones inventing and teaching these future A.I.s! So, if you're into tech and dreaming big, you could be a part of creating this fantastic future where A.I. helps us all live our best lives. The future of A.I. is about working together with machines to create a world that's even better than we can imagine!

Society, Ethics and A.I.

We've spent most of this book talking about why A.I. is so awesome and how it will soon be taking over the world. But is there a downside to all this awesomeness?

A lot of people think so. In fact, there are quite a few people who believe many of these Hollywood blockbuster movies about A.I. could come true (like *Terminator, the Matrix, A.I.,* and many more). That is, the possibility A.I. can evolve and become sentient (self-aware and conscious) and transform into an enemy of humanity when it realizes it no longer needs people. A.I. could literally arm itself with superior weapons, and since it is generally faster and more precise than humans when it comes to physical skills, we wouldn't stand much chance in an all-out war with A.I.-powered robots. Like a lot of these movies suggest, it's very possible that humans might become endangered species then. That is, if all of these assumptions that A.I. would somehow naturally want to dominate humans and take over the world were true. And, that's a pretty big "if."

This remotely possible outcome, is one reason why we're about to have a discussion on ethics. Considering that the scenario above is pretty unlikely, there are still many other good reasons to discuss the potential implications of technology like A.I..

The ethics behind new advanced technology developments has always been a hot button issue throughout time. One of the most common examples is nuclear energy. We're all aware that Einstein had a great deal to do with the development of many key concepts in atomic energy. Some of this knowledge was later used to develop nuclear bombs that destroyed major parts of Japan during the World War.

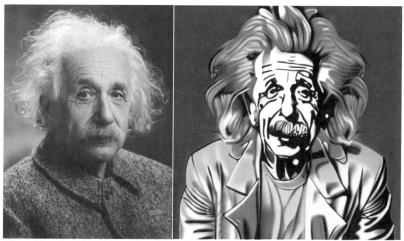
Albert Einstein, 1947 (left) Albert Einstein, reimagined by Stable Diffusion, 2024 (right)

However, nuclear energy is also considered a form of energy that can help alleviate climate change, which is becoming a bigger problem year after year, because of the use of fossil fuels. By and large, nuclear waste and environmental contamination is a very bad thing, and there have been major nuclear accidents like the famous ones at nuclear sites in Chernobyl, Russia, and Fukushima, Japan. But at the same time, today's renewable energy technologies just aren't enough to power the world's needs. Sustainable energy such as solar and wind energy would be the best solution to combat climate change, but it's just not very efficient or readily available everywhere. And, takes up a lot of space. Nuclear energy is seen by many people as a way to help power the world's energy needs for a while, until fully renewable energy can take over. There are many pros and cons regarding nuclear technology, but should the technology have never been invented? Would the world be better off without it? Or should the world simply use this powerful technology as wisely and carefully as possible? And, only use the technology for good reasons?

It's very much the same concern that the world has with A.I.. Are we at a point, so close to having extremely powerful A.I., that is capable of passing the Turing test, that we should worry about moving too fast? Should we hit the pause button on new A.I. development until we understand its potentials better? This is a question for all of you reading this book, since A.I. will experience some of its greatest growth during your generation. So, it's something you might want to think about, while you're working through the activities on the website resource links we've provided at the end of the book.

Economy & happiness:

One question a lot of people ask is, with all this technology development, will I lose my job? Will it be the case that there is no need for human workers, or human artists or musicians, since A.I. can pretty much do it all for us? Maybe even better than us?

This is something on everybody's minds. That, not only might A.I. take away their chance at earning income, but the very things that make us human might be done by A.I. without the need for any human involvement at all. It can all seem pretty depressing. But if there's one thing we know, is that history has a habit of repeating itself, and we can look to the past, to help us frame the future.

When the first wave of the industrial revolution ramped up in the late 1700's to early 1800's, people were worried that they would lose their jobs as factories opened up. River-powered textile factories, cotton gins, and steam powered machines threatened to create new efficiencies on such a scale that people worried they might soon all lose their jobs, which were mostly performed by hand from home at the time. Jobs that were previously done by skillful people, could now be done by machines at a constant and predictable pace, faster and in many cases, better, than humans. While some would argue that the industrialization of society is what has caused so many of today's global woes, it is also the reason for most of the advances in technology that make our lives so much better. While some jobs were indeed immediately lost, entirely new industries along with new types of jobs were created, and industry, in 4 separately defined periods, has continued to boom. Industrialization and technology innovation has gone hand in hand over the past few hundred years, ushering in improvements across numerous fields, ranging from transportation to agriculture to health and hygiene. During that time, human life expectancy has gone from the young 30's to well into the 70's.

Furthermore, the Human Development Index (HDI) which measures various human quality of life factors (education, standard of living, longevity), has shown steady increases in all regions of the world in that same timeframe.

Basically, according to the HDI, life is good, and it keeps getting better– and a lot of that has to do with the continued development of technology. After so many recent high tech innovations, including semiconductors and computing, the Internet, and advanced robotics, the world has been poised for new growth.

The big steel and oil barons of the past have become the tech entrepreneurs of today. Microsoft Oracle, Facebook, Google, Amazon and many other software / Internet software companies are all valued in the hundreds of billions of dollars; Google passed a trillion dollars in value in 2020. Not very long ago, Intel, Apple and others in the semiconductor and hardware space were the leaders in the computer sector. Nvidia (which was known for making video game products), has focused on A.I. in recent years. And, because of this, it has become one of the top valued companies in the world. It is becoming clear that new innovations and wealth have been created at a steadily increasing pace, and will continue to be created in the A.I. space.

But big money isn't everything. All that newly created value won't do any good if new technology doesn't raise the individual wealth of everybody in society, or at least make people happier. One thing's for sure, after all these periods of industrialization, and the creation of lots of new technology, people didn't lose their jobs, and they didn't get severely depressed. The development of new technologies like electronics created new products like laptops, cellphones and video game consoles—things that we humans enjoy, and that have created new jobs for us, in all sorts of brand new related industries. Industries that never existed before, but were created entirely from this new technology. Like A.I. has the potential to do, too.

Safety concerns:

With A.I. now being integrated into self-driving cars, and being tested throughout the world, there is a real possibility that sometime in the very near future, you may look in the window next to you and see nobody in the driver's seat. Of course, at the moment, most of the testing of these cars requires a human backup driver to sit in the front of the car. However, it's only a matter of time before this all changes.

There's even discussion of self-driving trucks, and there are now companies already looking at this and making major investments. Part of the reason for that is that nowadays, especially given the COVID pandemic, people tend to order goods and have them shipped to their homes, rather than go out to stores. Regardless, moving all these goods across the world doesn't just take ships, trains and planes, but lots and lots of trucks. Since trucks share the roads with cars, but they weigh twenty times more (a truck could weigh 80,000 pounds while a car might weigh only 4,000), they pose a real threat to safety in the event of a crash. Especially since the number of trucks on the road is on the rise. And once both cars and trucks go fully artificially intelligent, buses and other forms of shared transportation won't be too far behind.

With news of accidents already occurring in self-driving vehicles, it has many people wondering if A.I. driven vehicles are safe. And, since they are essentially driven by robots, would they value human or other animal life? If a self-driving truck sees a child running across the road, but there isn't time to stop, what would it do? If it's only programmed to brake and not run off the road in order to save a life at the expense of destroying the entire vehicle, would the A.I. make the right decision? Would it even know what to do? Now, what if instead of a truck, it's

an A.I.-powered schoolbus full of young students? Would it still take the risky choice, to run off the road, if it could endanger all the lives of the many children on board? What decision is the right one, in this case? At the moment, these are all very big questions that people are trying to answer. But, if the questions are never raised, people won't come up with answers to them. And that is precisely why it's important to discuss the ethical implications of the decision making powers that we will be programming into future A.I. applications.

Bias:

We mentioned earlier the concept of bias in the formulas behind neural networks. But in the human world, our sense of bias is a bit different. The word bias often brings up other words like prejudice and stereotypes and discrimination. And in today's society, we all know there is no place for bias. People should be treated equally and fairly. But, what we are seeing lately is a dangerous trend of many common A.I. applications becoming biased. Sometimes, the bias somehow innocently works its way into systems due to the way that society builds and structures its data. But sometimes, there are actual human biases that enter A.I. systems, from various sources, and the biases become integrated into the A.I. applications we use everyday. These applications are such a part of our lives, that it can be hard to change these systems as they grow larger and are used by more people over time. That's why its important to address and recognize these issues early on. Many people have noticed that certain facial recognition apps have biases in the sense that they work better for people of a certain gender or race than others. There is also evidence that criminal and law enforcement databases that use A.I. also have biases against minorities, or against people from certain neighborhoods. This can be a very serious issue if a face recognition or other system were to falsely identify someone as a criminal, and put his or her life in jeopardy for no good reason at all.

And the concern is not primarily about race or gender. Lately, there has been a lot of news that programs in smartphones have the potential to learn information about your interests, spending habits and even your bank account, through the A.I. that is integrated into these programs.

Imagine a world where people or companies can have a bias against you based on the things you like, or even your political views. Nobody would be safe from this sort of bias.

The potential for bad outcomes from A.I. bias are limitless. It's pretty scary. That's why over the past few years, many top companies have specifically recognized A.I. bias as a major potential problem and have invested a lot of money to try to nip it in the bud. Since so much A.I. is human-focused, and has so much to do with our personal identities, it's critical to make sure that A.I. can't make a mistake when it comes to who we are, especially if it makes these mistakes due to an inherent or a human-caused bias.

Decision-making:

As A.I. starts to become integrated not only into the products we use, and the cars we drive, and the apps in our phones, it is also steadily becoming part of our government. The cornerstone of democracy is the rule of law, and it is important to be able to enforce laws fairly and equally. All people, regardless of their personal backgrounds, or how much money they have, need to obey the law. And, to be fair, the justice system has to treat everybody the same. However, according to a research project conducted recently, it was found that judges who oversee bail hearings (whether or not a prisoner can be released temporarily) have biases in their decisions, based merely on the time of day. Judges in these particular bail hearing courts were found to give out the most favorable decisions early in the morning, or after lunch. So, that means, simply because the judges were well-fed and in a better mood, that some potential criminals received bail and others, right before lunch or at the end of the work day, didn't. Well, that certainly seems very unfair and completely biased—towards food!

In that case, would it better to have an A.I. judge, that is capable of weighing all the evidence and comparing each case fairly to other judicial decisions that have been made in the past? A judge-robot that doesn't get hungry and doesn't have any personal biases? Or is there the chance that the programmers behind the system may have unknowingly integrated some of their own personal biases into the system? How can an A.I. system like that be trusted?

Data scientists are looking at this very problem right now, and how A.I. might be used as a means of making intelligent decisions in an automated way that is fair to everybody. A.I. is already used in many standardized testing environments to take a first pass at reading over essays, and can serve as a gatekeeper between a college admissions office's decision to accept or deny an applicant. Some people think this is unfair, because maybe a person might interpret all the information different from the way a machine would. What would you prefer—an A.I. decision or a human one?

These issues and more are things we all need to consider, as both users and creators of A.I. technology, now, and well into the future. Far before we encounter potential issues.

One thing's for sure, A.I. is definitely already a part of our society, and the development of new A.I. technology is happening at a pace faster than many people could have ever imagined. Whether we love A.I., accept A.I. or hate A.I., it's coming our way, no matter what. So it's important that we don't waste any time, since we all need to GET READY FOR A.I.!

Glossary

- **Algorithms**: These are step-by-step instructions that computers follow to solve problems. NLP algorithms help computers understand language.

- **Applications**: The practical uses of NLP technology. These include tasks like machine translation, chatbots, and text summarization.

- **Artificial Intelligence (A.I.)**: This is the field of computer science that creates intelligent machines capable of tasks typically requiring human intelligence.

- **Artificial Neural Networks**: These are computer systems modeled after the structure and function of the human brain. They play a role in some NLP models.

- **Comprehension**: This means being able to understand the meaning of something, like figuring out a complex news article. GPT can comprehend the meaning behind human language.

- **Context**: Imagine the background information that helps you understand a joke. Context is similar—it's the surrounding information that helps computers understand the meaning of language.

- **Deep Learning**: A subfield of machine learning that uses complex models inspired by the human brain. This is often used in advanced NLP applications.

- **Deforestation**: The process of cutting down or removing large areas of trees and forests. This can happen for various reasons, such as clearing land for farming, building cities, or harvesting wood for products like paper and furniture.

- **Generative Pre-trained Transformer (GPT)**: Think of GPT as a super-powered A.I. program trained on massive amounts of text data. It can then use this knowledge to create human-quality writing.

- **Informed**: "Informed" means having knowledge or information about a particular subject or situation. When you are informed, you have the facts and details you need to understand something or make a decision. For example, if you read the news every day, you are informed about what is happening in the world.

- **Life Expectancy**: The average number of years a person is expected to live. It's like making an educated guess about how long people in a certain place or time period will live based on their health, lifestyle, and other factors. For example, if the life expectancy in a country is 80 years, it means that on average, people there are expected to live to be 80 years old.

- **Machine Learning**: This is a type of A.I. where computers learn from data without needing programming. Machine learning is like teaching computers to learn from examples and improve on their own. NLP relies heavily on machine learning.

- **Minimally invasive**: "Minimally invasive" refers to a medical procedure or treatment that involves the smallest possible amount of cutting or damage to the body. It uses tiny cuts, small tools, and sometimes cameras to perform surgery or other treatments, which usually means less pain, a faster recovery, and smaller scars compared to traditional surgery.

- **Model**: Think of a computer program that learns from information and makes predictions. That's a model!

- **Natural Language Processing (NLP)**: Imagine teaching computers to understand our everyday language, like text messages and social media posts. NLP is the field that makes this possible!

- **Parameters**: Imagine the dials on a sound system you adjust for the perfect sound. Parameters in A.I. models are like those dials, helping them learn and improve.

- **Plasticity:** This refers to the ability of something to be easily shaped or molded. In biology, it describes the brain's capacity to change and adapt due to experience and learning. This ability enables the brain to reorganize itself by forming new neural connections throughout life.

- **Pre-trained**: Imagine studying really hard for a test beforehand. A pre-trained model is like that—it's been trained on a lot of data before being used for a specific task.

- **Redundancy**: having extra or backup systems to ensure something still works if the main system fails. For example, saving your work in multiple places to avoid losing it.

- **Reinforcement (Positive / Negative)**: Positive reinforcement in A.I. is when the system gets a reward or positive feedback for making a correct decision or performing well. For example, if an A.I. correctly identifies a cat in a photo, it might get a "point" or some other positive signal. This reward encourages the A.I. to keep making correct decisions. Negative reinforcement in A.I. is when something negative or a penalty is removed because the system made a correct decision or performed well. For instance, if an A.I. is penalized for making mistakes but then correctly identifies a cat in a photo, the penalty is reduced or removed. This encourages the A.I. to keep making correct decisions to avoid penalties.

  In both cases, reinforcement helps the A.I. learn and improve its behavior by encouraging correct actions.

- **Remarkable**: This means something is very impressive and worth noticing.
- **Transistor**: A semiconductor device used to amplify or switch electronic signals and power. It is a fundamental building block

of modern electronic devices, allowing for the control of electric currents in circuits. Transistors are essential in computers, smartphones, and many other electronic gadgets.

Resources Links

A few fun and useful A.I. resources:

Please note that in the fast paced world of A.I., sometimes technology gets updated or replaced quickly. If a resource below isn't working, please just go to your favorite search engine (Google is preferred) and search for the title of the resource to find a new/updated or equivalent link.

Teachable Machine
https://teachablemachine.withgoogle.com/

Magenta A.I. Music Demos
https://magenta.tensorflow.org/demos/

Nvidia A.I. Playground
https://www.nvidia.com/en-us/research/ai-playground/

Experiments with Google (A.I. Page)
https://labs.google/

Image Credits

p.6-7 background Image https://pixabay.com/vectors/cranium-head-human-male-man-2099083/

p.8-9 robot illustrations by Chen-hui Chang

p.13 https://en.wikipedia.org/wiki/Golem#/media/File:Prague-golem-reproduction.jpg (public domain)

p.24 abacus https://commons.wikimedia.org/wiki/File:Traditional_Chinese_abacus_illustrating_the_suspended_bead_use.jpg (public domain)

p.25 Bell punch adding machine (public domain) https://commons.wikimedia.org/wiki/File:Bell_Punch_506D_adding_machine_-_Ridai_Museum_of_Modern_Science,_Tokyo_-_DSC07529.JPG

p.26 https://commons.wikimedia.org/wiki/File:Computer_chips_circuits_boards.jpg (public domain, by Jon Sullivan)

p.27 CPU https://commons.wikimedia.org/wiki/File:Cpu_1.jpg (public domain by blickpixel from Pixabay)

p.28 a PC computer https://commons.wikimedia.org/wiki/File:Ibm_computer_pc_5150_(6049156797).jpg (public domain by Fried Dough)

p.31 Alan Turing https://en.wikipedia.org/wiki/Alan_Turing#/media/File:Alan_Turing_(1912-1954)_in_1936_at_Princeton_University.jpg (public domain)

p.32 Military Enigma Machine https://simple.wikipedia.org/wiki/Enigma_machine#/media/File:EnigmaMachineLabeled.jpg (public domain by Karsten Sperling)

p.32 https://commons.wikimedia.org/wiki/File:Wartime_picture_of_a_Bletchley_Park_Bombe.jpg (public domain)

p.33 https://commons.wikimedia.org/wiki/File:Old_drawing_of_

MIT.JPG (public domain by McGraw-Hill Pub. Co. (Albany, N.Y.))

p.34 Perceptron diagram https://commons.wikimedia.org/wiki/File:Perceptron-bias.svg (public domain)

p.36 https://commons.wikimedia.org/wiki/File:Raspberry-Pi-2-Bare-BR.jpg (public domain by Evan-Amos)

p.43 https://commons.wikimedia.org/wiki/File:Cube_With_Hidden_Lines.jpg (public domain by Tigerfarm1)

p.44 https://commons.wikimedia.org/wiki/File:LCD_pixels_RGB.jpg (public domain by Robnil01)

p.49 MartinThoma, CC0, via Wikimedia Commons, https://commons.wikimedia.org/wiki/File:Perceptron-unit.svg

p.50 https://commons.wikimedia.org/wiki/File:Die_of_the_first_555_chip.jpg (public domain by CQ Publishing Co., Ltd.)

p.53 Zufzzi, Public domain, via Wikimedia Commons, https://commons.wikimedia.org/wiki/File:Neural_network_bottleneck_achitecture.svg

p.58 Plate 38: Section of the Wirksworth Cave and Fossils https://www.c82.net/iconography/geognosy-geology ENGRAVER: HENRY WINKLES https://www.c82.net/iconography/about#licensing

p.58 thresholds identify fossil – Barnas Monteith

p.60 NOAA, Public domain, via Wikimedia Commons, https://commons.wikimedia.org/wiki/File:ClimateDashboard-global-sea-levels-graph-20230329-1400px.png

p.61 https://commons.wikimedia.org/wiki/File:S_%26_P_500.webp Wikideas1, public domain

p.61 Federal Reserve Bank, public domain https://commons.wikimedia.org/wiki/File:2022_Dow_Jones_Industrial_Average_and_S%26P_500.png

p.63 Ranged Ranger, CC0, via Wikimedia Commons, https://commons.wikimedia.org/wiki/File:LMMS_1.2.1_Demo.png

p.64 https://commons.wikimedia.org/wiki/File:12_Lead_EKG_ST_Elevation_tracing_color_coded.jpg (public domain)

p.69 Daderot, CC0, via Wikimedia Commons, https://commons.wikimedia.org/wiki/File:Kismet,_1993-2000,_view_2_-_MIT_Museum_-_DSC03711.JPG

p.77 Pleiotrope, Public domain, via Wikimedia Commons, https://commons.wikimedia.org/wiki/File:Protein_IL28RA_PDB_3OG4.png

p.82 https://commons.wikimedia.org/wiki/File:Albert_Einstein_Head.jpg (public domain)

p.86 https://commons.wikimedia.org/wiki/File:2003_IC_CE_model_schoolbus,_North_Syracuse,_New_York_(October_2007).jpg (public domain by Nsyrbus)

About the Author

A painterly A.I. Image of Barnas

Barnas Monteith, as a young student, was one of the top national record holders for first place science fair wins, for a project involving data science and predictive computer programs to study evolution. Over time, Barnas studied both science and engineering fields, and became an avid advocate for STEM education, serving in various government and non-profit leadership roles. He was the youngest and longest serving leader of the MIT Massachusetts State Science & Engineering Fair, working with numerous teachers and students on A.I. science projects. He spent a number of years doing research at Harvard and MIT, notably on award winning project using A.I. to predict medical outcomes. He is the cofounder of several technology companies, and spent many years developing and producing products for the semiconductor industry, helping to make planarization tools for some of today's most advanced computer chips. He has published numerous scholarly papers (and other books) on a range of science and technology topics, especially A.I., and regularly presents about A.I., semitech and other STEM fields at conferences and invited lectures around the world.